THE
RICHNESS
OF
DIVORCE

7 STEPS
TO UNWIND YOUR
MARRIAGE WITH
LOVE AND GRACE

SYLVIA GUINAN, MBA, CDFA

FLOWER *of* LIFE PRESS

For information about this title or to order other books and/or electronic media, contact the publisher: Astara@floweroflifepress.com

To reach the author:
Sylvia Guinan Enterprises, LLC
sylviaguinan.com
therichnessofdivorce@sylviaguinan.com

Cover and Interior design: 1106 Design

Cover Artwork: Elenora Ferraggatta, www.elenoraferragatta.com

Library of Congress Control Number: Available upon request.

ISBN: 978-1-7349730-3-7

Printed in the United States of America

DEDICATION

This book is dedicated to the individuals who have the courage and strength to learn how to navigate their divorce process with love and grace.

It is also dedicated to my three beautiful, loving, and resilient children, Grayson, Olivia, and Sophia, who have taught me so much about love, life, purpose, and acceptance as I navigated through my own divorce. They inspire me daily with their grit and keen ability to go with the flow.

"I have gotten to know Sylvia personally and professionally over the past six years. Through her book, Sylvia teaches anyone going through the difficult divorce process how to stay grounded and how to keep moving forward on the right track. Divorce is a major life event and unusually immersed in negativity. Sylvia guides you through the process with the utmost grace and positive direction. She is the ultimate when it comes to practicing what you preach."

—KENNETH J. PIA, CPA, ABV, ASA, MCBA

"Within her book, *The Richness of Divorce*, Sylvia Guinan recognizes the necessity of personal responsibility, unconditional love, and a desire to keep the big picture in mind while also lovingly, and with grace, remembering who you are. Understanding your emotions, your reactions and your actions allows you to have the inner strength needed to confront the fears, anger, and uncertainties that are a natural process of letting go and coming alive in a far more vibrant, alive, and wise form. This book is a must-read for those who have completed their divorce as well as those who are in the process. We are never done learning and growing."

—DOROTHY A. MARTIN-NEVILLE, PhD

CONTENTS

INTRODUCTION

Because I have a choice, I choose love.
—DEEPAK CHOPRA

When you observe a tree, you can connect with the many realities of the human experience. Trees exist in two worlds—they take root and establish a foundation underground, and, at the same time, they use that foundation to grow and thrive above the earth. The roots are grounded and represent the growth and foundation that has formed throughout the years. The roots are in the soil, and we cannot see how deep or wide they have grown, but we are certain that they go deep and are strong, since they are holding the tree up. The leaves and branches are visible, and you can see how they are affected by the seasons and daily climate, just as we are impacted by the seasons of our life. You can use nature and its magic as the key to opening the door to your unique story.

One of the lyrics in a Jewel song resonates with me. *"Nature has a funny way of breaking what does not bend."* As you go through your divorce, you will use your roots to keep you grounded and strong. Your branches and leaves will potentially grow and thrive, and the ones that no longer serve you will break off as you navigate through your divorce. This book is going to provide you with the power of perspective and it will empower you to see that you can choose how to navigate through the process of divorce with love and grace so that branches and leaves grow and flourish. You have more power than you know. You have the power to choose love and grace as you proceed with unwinding your marriage and embarking upon your new beginning. Everything you experience in life starts with intention. Intention is what you focus your energy on. You have a choice about where you decide to focus your intention during your divorce process. The key to this is awareness.

Your branches can only reach high if your roots go deep.
—BRIAN LOQUE

Have you ever stopped to observe the ocean—to really observe what is going on with its never-ending movement and flow? There are days when the water is calm and it resembles glass. Calm weather normally contributes to stillness in the sea. During stormy days, the waves are normally bigger and crash more aggressively upon the sand. Think about floating on top of the ocean during stormy weather or rough seas. What would happen? You would get tossed around, sometimes crashing onto the sand, only to get sucked back into the water. Seconds later, you would be thrust onto the sand again. You would feel a bit out of control and at the mercy of the sea. However, the deeper you dive into the ocean, what happens? There is more calmness and peace. The waves are not banging around down there, rather, there is a calmer and more-peaceful flow. Regardless of the weather, your flow will be more consistent and peaceful when you go deeper. Therefore, the deeper and more peaceful you are during your transition, the more control you will have as you navigate through challenging emotions and difficult days. As you embark on one of the most difficult life-altering experiences, you can decide if you will allow yourself to get banged around or if you will choose calmness and peace. Even though you will be dealing with outside emotions and difficult days, you can decide to move forward through your divorce with peace. Even if your partner is angry and hurtful, you have the power to go deep and stay in the calm and peaceful waters of the transition. You have more control than you know. My hope is that you decide to go deep and get through this difficult process with love and grace.

In divorce, being your best self is critical. You have the power and inner strength to navigate through the divorce process with love and grace; it is all about perspective. Focus on what you can control. You do not need to carry with you the negative stories or the negative messages you have from your partner/spouse. Take control by no longer blaming your spouse for the negative messages or situations that occurred. Make an effort to get quiet and go deep. Acknowledge both the positive and negative situations that came out of the relationship. Then, stay deep, decide which stories or messages no longer serve you, and let them go. If you decide to hold onto those messages, you will become the item floating on top of the sea, being tossed around and sucked in by the waves and tossed back out over and over again. You have the choice to stay on the surface, which will cause more unnecessary suffering. Decide to go deep and to experience the gentle flow with peace and control. One of the most powerful ways to accomplish this is connecting with your chakras.

You cannot always control what goes on outside.
But you can always control what goes on inside.
—WAYNE DYER

Chakras are the energy points located throughout the body believed to be centers of spiritual power. It is here that energy can flow through us to empower and strengthen us. The chakras can easily become unbalanced as you navigate through your divorce. There are seven chakras, ranging from the top of your head to the base of your spine. Tapping into your chakras and keeping them aligned and flowing is a healthy and powerful way to navigate through your divorce process. By nourishing your chakras one at a time, you can become physically, mentally, and spiritually stronger. When you become aware of and in tune with these energetic power centers, you will find yourself feeling increased clarity of thought, more self-confidence, enhanced communication skills, and a deeper sense of inner peace.

It is easy for your chakras to become blocked as you are navigating through divorce. This is the worst possible time to have your chakras blocked, as you need all the strength and empowerment within you to get through this draining process. If the energy of any of these chakras becomes blocked, your emotional and physical health can suffer. This book illustrates how you can use tools to open your chakras during different phases of your divorce. My hope is that you will be able to tap into your chakras and make sure they are aligned as you go through your divorce journey. Throughout the book, I will illustrate examples of how you may choose to use different chakras for different stages of your transition.

Think about what happens when you are contemplating making a change. An idea comes into your head, a thought that perhaps a different direction is needed. These new ideas come from Crown Chakra energy. They include enlightenment, freedom, and connection to something greater than yourself. As your mind starts to focus on your idea, your new path, you start to use your Third Eye Chakra, which is composed of energy, vision, and intuition. Once you become clear that this is the right path and you communicate your intentions to your partner/spouse, you are using the Throat Chakra energy, speaking truth and life purpose. Then you take it to your heart, using your Heart Chakra energy, which deals with energy, transformation, and love. Next, you begin to implement the change into reality, using your Solar Plexus Chakra energy, power and wisdom. Then you proceed to water (nourish) your new reality using your Sacral Chakra energy, until finally it *is* your new reality and takes concrete form. That is your Root Chakra energy, which deals with balance, grounding, and presence.

As you navigate through your transition, it is important that you find ways to get quiet and calm so you can create the peace from within. By getting quiet, you can also connect with the areas that need your attention. Some ways that we connect with ourselves in a healthy way is being in nature, doing yoga, meditating and participating in activities that bring us calmness and peace. It is important to nurture yourself during this time. As busy as you get, it is essential that you make the time to take care of yourself in order to heal in a healthy way. It will also be necessary so that you can bring your best self to this challenging situation.

Everyone, even the most powerful and strong among us, at their deepest core wants to get through their divorce with love and grace. In the middle of writing this book, an author friend of mine was in town; we spent time discussing the message I wanted to convey in this book. Wanting to make the most of our time, I offered to take her to the airport on her last day. During the ride, she shared with me that my book would move many people going through the divorce process. Right before I dropped her off, I noticed a state trooper driving behind me. I found it interesting that, as I dropped her off, he pulled over. I was hoping this was just a coincidence. As I began to drive out of the airport, he pulled out right behind me. Within 30 seconds, I saw those dreaded lights go on, and I immediately pulled over. He approached the car and asked the usual question: "Do you know why I am pulling you over?" Of course, I had my suspicions but decided to let him tell me, minimizing the risk of my adding to his list. He proceeded to tell me my registration was expired. "I am so sorry, officer. I am recently divorced, and I apparently dropped the ball on that one, I explained." He responded, with an intrigued look on his face, "How long?" I responded with what I thought was a coy response: "My expired registration, or how long have I been divorced?" He surprised me with his response: "How long did it take?" Then I thought I would be humorous and asked, "How long did my divorce take?" I was waiting for a chuckle, but he responded, "Yes—how long did the process take? I am currently starting my process and was wondering what I should expect." I responded that I was able to have my divorce completed within three months of filing.

I proceeded to tell him that my focus and my goal were to get through it with love and grace. His response was, "I want that." We proceeded to talk for a while, and I was amazed at how this very strong man with a gun, cuffs, and a club had so much love and compassion. He was open to discussing his situation, and he didn't want to fight or battle, rather he clearly wanted to get through the process with love and grace. I feel, in my heart of hearts, that we all have a tender part in our soul, and we all want to get through this painful process with love and grace as opposed to producing collateral damage. I also feel the universe is always sending us a message, and I got mine loud and clear. I thought about our conversation for the next forty-five minutes during my ride home. There are no coincidences: the universe was giving me a message; my author friend was correct, and there is an audience who really needs to hear how one can navigate divorce with love and grace.

My hope is that you will be able to take some things you learn from this book and apply them to your situation. It is certainly one of the most painful and difficult processes to navigate through, but you have so much control over your experience. How you choose to look at your situation will affect how you get through the process. Instead of asking yourself, "Why is this happening *to* me?" ask, "Why is this happening *for* me?" If you ask the question and replace the word "to" with the word "for," you go from being a victim to being an active participant who can embrace an experience that is meant to lead you to your next step in your journey. We will explore how your transition can go from being a *loss* to being a new, limitless *beginning*.

Allow hope to be your guide. Hope and fear cannot occupy the same space, so, open up to hope, and invite it to stay as you navigate through your process. Hope has enormous power. We will need to have hope as we navigate through the divorce process, which is full of emotions and uncertainty. Learn to embrace the uncertainty, and trust that there is growth and wisdom that will come after the chaos has passed. Passive hope will not be effective for you—it will be an excuse for you to do nothing. Make your hope active, and connect it to your wishes.

Select your thoughts the way you select your clothes, with thoughtfulness and intention. Give up judgment, not only of your spouse but also of yourself. Stop waiting for your soon-to-be ex to forgive you, and, instead, forgive yourself. Forgive yourself for letting go, and forgive yourself for hanging on too long. Forgiveness is the biggest lesson in this journey. If you cannot forgive, you will harm yourself as the negative energy builds up overtime. Learn to forgive so that you can find the peace and calmness you deserve.

The only way to truly heal is to trust. Believe in love again. Learn to trust that you are on the right path and that things will unfold as they should. When you set out to help yourself, you help everybody around you. It is not selfish to honor what you need. Set your dreams and goals, and then release them to the universe, along with any attachment that you may have to the outcome. Learn to go with the flow.

STEP 1

FIND YOUR TRUTH

Sahasrara ❀ Crown Chakra

LOCATION: *Crown of the head*

COLOR: *Violet/Clear White*

STONE: *Amethyst*

OIL: *Blue Lotus*

SOUND: *This chakra is beyond sound*

THEME: *Enlightenment*

HEALING PROPERTY: *Spiritual Understanding*

GIFT: *Wisdom*

LIFE ISSUE: *Attachment*

ARCHETYPE: *Sage/Guru*

he Crown Chakra opens during those times in your life when you are facing difficult personal choices. These challenges often bring you a stronger connection to spirit, a greater understanding of what you are capable of, and an insight into what your higher purpose in life might be. The goal as you navigate through the divorce process is to allow yourself to connect with spirit on a deeper level and to trust that you are here to be happy and fulfill your soul's longing for love, peace, joy, and meaningful connections. When your Crown Chakra does open, you will find yourself needing more rest, tranquility, and peace in order to gain the strength you need to navigate through your transition.

The Crown Chakra, or "Thousand Petal Lotus," is the chakra at the top of your head. Wisdom, understanding, and spiritual connection flow down from this chakra. This is the chakra that connects you to the universe and to others. Focus on this chakra to work toward enlightenment and freedom, and to connect to something bigger than yourself. This chakra also allows you to tune into the wisdom beyond your sensory realm. This chakra connects you to individual awareness and infinite consciousness.

"Why is that voice in my head constantly pointing out that I am not happy in this relationship?"

"It is going to be okay. Things will get better."

"Is it really that bad? Bad enough to break up my family?"

"How can I even consider putting my family through a divorce?"

"Will I ever be happy?"

"Am I being selfish?"

"If I do more, he/she will turn around."

"I don't want to be married to someone who can *live with me*—I want to be married to someone who *can't live without me.*"

Have you ever had that internal dialogue? For many of us, this conversation has gone on for years and years. We are masters of quieting our voice and suppressing our feelings, particularly when the stakes are so high. The hardest part of the divorce process is admitting the truth to yourself.

We cannot change anything until we accept it.
—CARL JUNG

OWNING YOUR TRUTH

It is painful and scary to admit that you are simply no longer satisfied in your marriage. It may seem overwhelming to entertain the idea that what looks to everyone like a pretty picture is not as it appears. You may even try to convince yourself for a while that it *is* as pretty as it appears, but, in time, your heart will keep pulling at you until you have to face the facts. Things will start to happen, and patterns will become more obvious until you can no longer hide from the truth. You may start to experience a lack of connection and intimacy. You may feel lonelier when you are with your partner than when you are alone. You may even start to question if you're ever going to be able to feel something for your partner again. These are all signs that you need to focus on your relationship. At that point, you must decide either to put your all into working through those issues or into trying to figure out how you can begin the process of accepting your truth.

There will be times when you feel that you and your spouse are starting to drift apart; you'll begin to realize that you have different interests. As long as there is no resentment, animosity, or conflict, you can navigate through this and work to find some common ground. When you and your partner are on different paths, and resentment, animosity, and conflict arise, this is when the relationship begins to deteriorate. If you do not address this over time, in the long run, you are not only *lacking what you need* from your relationship—it starts to *cost* you. You start to lose yourself.

The mind replays what the heart cannot delete.

What it really boils down to is being able to look honestly and deeply into your relationship with your partner and your relationship with yourself. If your relationship looks great from the outside, but from the inside, it is not serving you, it will begin to chisel away at your authentic self. When you lose connection with self, that is damaging to you. You perceive only things that *you* think exist. Therefore, it is imperative that you own your truth. You must face the situation that exists, not the situation you *wish* existed. Do not get stuck in a box. There are many other options.

WHICH VOICE IS SPEAKING MY TRUTH?

It is challenging to distinguish between the two voices in your head that you are hearing in your head. One voice coming from your mind is based on constructs we have created, such as good or bad, right or wrong. Another, opposing voice comes from your soul, your spirit. A good tool to use when deciphering these inner voices is to ask, "Who is talking to me now? Is it my mind (ego), or is it my soul (heart)?" One good way to check is understanding that the mind operates on constructs that are based on judgments. So, if the essence of the voice is fear-based, it's normally coming from the mind. When the voice is more love-based, it is coming from the heart. Learn to love from your mind and think from your heart.

So, how do you decide which voice inside your head is telling you the truth? Which voice is really coming from your higher self? How do you really know if staying in the marriage or divorce is the best path for you? First, you have to start by promising to be a hundred percent truthful to yourself as you navigate the process. It is one of the hardest truths to face. But you have to face it. You owe it to yourself *and* to your partner.

It is important that you focus time and energy on getting to your truth. You will most likely try to avoid it, but the more time you spend getting quiet and listening to your soul, your spirit, the clearer the truth will become. Another way to get to your truth is to ask yourself questions—lots of questions. Keeping a journal with your questions and answers will also help you navigate to your truth. Working with a psychologist, therapist, or divorce coach can help accelerate the process and give you a safe place for coming to terms with your truth and planning your next steps.

It is important that you explore every option to save your marriage before you decide to move forward with a divorce. Divorce should truly be a last step, when the marriage is truly irreconcilable. My suggestion is to keep the lines of communication open as much as you can. Allow yourself to be vulnerable and come from a loving place. Avoid placing blame; change your language from "You always do xyz" to "When you do xyz, it makes me feel hurt and vulnerable." Ask for what you need from the relationship, and also ask your spouse what they need. It can be helpful to work with a professional who is a neutral party, such as a marriage therapist or relationship coach. Take the focus off labeling things as "right" or "wrong," "good" or "bad," but rather be open to what currently *is*, to how you got there, and to looking at ways to make changes to salvage the marriage.

The situation is much greater than "right" or "wrong," and labeling will never resolve the conflict. The bottom line is that each of you need something you are not currently getting from the relationship. It can be love, compassion, caring, support, kindness, partnership, intimacy, patience, understanding, etc. Once you each know what it is that you need, it is up to both parties to do their best to give that to the other. Even if you already think you *are* providing this to your partner, they are not feeling it. So, change it up, and offer what they need in a different way.

*I will never regret you or say I wish I'd never met you,
because once upon a time, you were exactly
what I needed.*

A wise friend of mine once said, "If you boil down marriages and why they do not work, regardless of the different stories that got them to this place, the bottom line is this: a woman wants to feel loved, and a man wants to feel respected.

The minute one of those things goes missing, the breakdown of the relationship begins."

If you determine there is no way to save the marriage—or if your spouse is the one who wants to end it—decide how you want to go through this transition. Yes, *decide*. You do have a choice. You can decide to make it as difficult and painful as possible, or you can decide to come from a place of peace and set your intentions to navigate through the process with love and grace. Your partner may not cooperate at first—or, regrettably, ever—but you can decide to stay in that more loving and positive space.

WHEN THE ONLY THING MORE IMPOSSIBLE THAN LEAVING IS STAYING

You don't want to hurt anyone. It's not that you can't have it easy; it's just that you can't have it so hard. The thought of ending your relationship creates anxiety. The anxiety stems from not knowing if you are making the right decision. How do you take the next step—a step you know will hurt your spouse and potentially your children? Staying will hurt you. Are you willing to accept the consequences? How do you decide if a relationship is too bad to stay in or not bad enough to leave?

There is no such thing as a guilt-free, painless option that will be executed exactly at the right time. None of those things exist when you decide to leave your marriage.

My yoga teacher said, "You are either honoring yourself or ignoring what your soul, your spirit, needs." The heaviness of the fear can be overbearing at times. Remember what we talked about in the Introduction: fear and hope cannot occupy the same space; focus on choosing hope. Sometimes it will feel like blind hope, but just close your eyes, and go with it. When you are making your decision, do not look through your head—look through your heart. At some point, when you get really quiet and listen, you will start to feel a sense of hope and direction. There will come a time when the discomfort that comes from not making a change will outweigh the fear of making one.

No longer lend your strength to that which
you wish to be free from.
—Jewel

If you are the one who is deciding to leave the marriage but cannot bear the guilt that comes with that decision, I challenge you to look at your situation through a different lens. Think of it from this perspective: your partner deserves to be chosen. Your partner deserves to be with someone who will love them unconditionally for who they are. If you are not serving this need, you may be doing your partner a favor by opening up the opportunity for your partner to meet someone who can fill that need. If your partner is leaving you, consider the fact that *you* deserve to be chosen, and, if they are not choosing you, they are doing you a service by leaving.

HOW DO YOU WORK WITH YOUR CROWN CHAKRA TO GET THROUGH THE SEPARATION PROCESS WITH LOVE AND GRACE?

Whether you decide to unwind your marriage or your partner decides to unwind the marriage, it is important that you open up your relationship to spirit immediately. You first need to make peace with your circumstances and encourage yourself to understand that there is a purpose for everything. Trust that there is a reason that this is taking place. Spirit has a path for you. It is key to get very quiet during this time and listen; you need to connect with spirit and what it is guiding you to do. Trust that spirit is guiding you, and stay connected to self. The *mind* will bring up all sorts of fears and insecurities. It is only trying to protect you, but you must understand that it is your *soul*, your *spirit* which will truly guide you to your life's purpose and the next step.

If you believe it will work out, you will see
the opportunities. If you believe it won't,
you will see the obstacles.
—WAYNE DYER

This is a scary time, and often people rely on or turn to faith because they need to trust blindly. Know that you will be okay. Spirit did not put you here to suffer. Spirit put you here because this chapter is coming to an end and no longer serves you or your partner. If you choose to ignore spirit, you will experience the feather-to-boulder effect that my dear friend Anne often talks about. The feather is when you get the gentle reminder that your current situation is no longer serving you. Your soul agrees, but your mind tells you that you are crazy, that it will be fine, and that you should stop causing issues. If you choose to ignore the feather, you will eventually get a slap in the face, which causes you to admit to yourself and to select friends and family that a change will be necessary in the not-so-distant future. The issue is that the mind steps in and tells you why this is a terrible thing to put yourself, your spouse, and your family through. The mind will tell you that you are

11

not strong enough to succeed or that you will not be able to get through this situation.

If you ignore the situation, then, in the not-so-distant future, comes the boulder through the windshield. The unfortunate thing about the boulder is that you no longer can be proactive in making the change but are now in reactive mode. Change is scary, and fear of the unknown can be paralyzing if you allow it to be. This is your time to deepen your relationship with spirit and to trust that you will be okay. Understand that it is a very difficult decision, but if you get out in front of it bravely, you can get through it with love and grace. If you wait for the boulder to hit, you will be acting out of shock, fear, anger, and resentment, as opposed to clarity, confidence, control, love, and grace.

You can choose courage, or you can choose comfort.
You cannot have both.
—BRENE BROWN

Life is all about perspective, and you can look at your situation through one of two different lenses.

1. The "poor me" lens will leave you feeling like the victim. "Why is this happening **to me**?" This scenario causes you to view your divorce as a failure; you have negative feelings for your soon-to-be ex and blame them for the demise of your marriage. This scenario leaves you feeling hopeless, angry, and resentful.

2. The "new possibility" lens will allow you to ask, "Why is this happening **for me**?" You ground yourself in hope and trust that you will be okay. There is room for only one emotion, either hope or fear—you decide. Look at your former relationship, honor the good things that served you, and understand that it is now time to lovingly and gracefully end it. This is not a failure but rather a relationship that has run its course, and now it is time for a new beginning. With a sense of faith and trust, know that spirit will always be by your side to guide you as you prepare for your new life to come.

When you trust and surrender to self, your spirit will sustain you, guide you, and open doors that will lead you to greater fulfillment and a deeper sense of purpose. We all need to understand that life is a journey, and, at some point or another, we have to get off the road we are on, either by choice or circumstance, in order to reach our ultimate destination. Often the road less traveled is the most scenic and beautiful. The reason we are afraid to explore it is that it is not as safe as the paved road with marked signs. It is rocky, muddy, woody, and sometimes treacherous; it may even lack guardrails. But once you arrive, you will see the beauty and thank yourself. Divorce is taking the road less traveled. It is going to be rocky, muddy, scary, sad, and, sometimes, treacherous as you go through your transition. I have seen the strongest of the strong crumble at first, but I have also seen many come out the other side and say, "There is so much light at the end."

The light at the end comes from many different sources. The first is that, if you honor yourself through the process and allow yourself to be vulnerable, you will be brave and explore your new, true beliefs about life and your new future. The key as you go through the process is not to accept what has been *taught* to you about divorce and separation but rather to *create* the new norm that is right for you and your family.

MY STORY:

When I was trying to figure out what the best path was for me, I promised myself that no immediate change would be required. I saw the first step as just telling myself the truth and sitting with it. The way to get to the truth is to get quiet. Meditation is a wonderful tool. I found I was struggling with being still and quiet so much that I committed to forty days of consecutive yoga, a New Year's program my yoga studio was launching. Every Monday, after an hour-and-fifteen-minute hot yoga class, we would sit in a circle and share. It wasn't until day thirty-six that I got my answer. The teacher asked us, "Do you love yourself?" I was so delighted as I had heard my inner voice screaming "Yes!" only to find, a few seconds later, my soul asking me, "If you love me, why are you keeping me in this marriage? Why are you ignoring my voice telling you what I need?"

It was a very powerful moment. Part of me wanted to cry because I felt that I finally had direction that was coming from my authentic self, my heart, my soul. The other part of me wanted to cry because I could not fathom how I would proceed with this terrifying new path. I remember coming home and feeling like I was being fake by hiding such a big, life-altering secret from my spouse and my children. As time progressed, it became harder and more painful to hold back my truth.

My inner circle, my friends who knew what my intentions were, would gently ask me, "When are you going to make your move?" I would always, without skipping a beat, share why now was not a good time but that my intentions were to do it, to move forward. Finally, one night, my friend Dr. Dorothy, invited me over for a glass of wine. As I was relaxing on her couch, sipping my wine, and sharing stories with her, I heard a knock at the door. Surprisingly, my friend, Anne, had decided to stop over also. Suddenly the questions were coming at me from both my friends: "When are you going to tell him?" "How will you do it?" In my usual fashion, I responded, "I am going to do it when the time is right."

The tone of our casual conversation turned, and they both started saying, "You are never going to do it! Why don't you admit you want to remain in an unhappy situation?" Trying to hang on to my usual response, I replied, "I will do it in a couple of months after . . ." I was immediately interrupted. "Sylvia, honey," Doctor Dorothy and Anne said, "there is *never* a 'right' time. There will always be a reason to wait. There will never be a good time to deliver the news to your spouse and your children."

I felt my heartbeat immediately start to race. I felt a little cornered, but rightfully so. I do like to face my truth and honor friends who are willing to hold up the mirror. "Okay," I finally said. "I will do it."

It was hard to tell my spouse, although I don't feel he was totally surprised. I had been asking for what I needed and expressing my concerns for many years. Telling my children is the hardest thing I have ever done. Even though I had been contemplating whether I should stay in the marriage for more than six years, I knew my decision would come as a shock to my family. Seeing the looks on their faces was, by far, the hardest and most painful thing I have ever experienced.

Fast forward to today. All three of my children are resilient, confident, happy, grounded, and, most importantly, they know they are loved by both of their parents. We told them that the only major change for them was that they were going from one loving household to two loving households. My ex-husband and I treat each other with kindness and respect, and we make it extremely easy for the kids to be around both of us. Our messaging has and will always be, "The marriage did not work, but the family will always work." Let's face it—those kids are part of both of us, and we both need to honor our history and the roles we play moving forward in the lives of our children.

My sister, Lydia, passed away many years ago. It was a tragic loss for me. I ended up seeing a healer to help me navigate through the process. The healer was quite gifted and helped immensely. I remember a prayer she suggested I say daily. I have said it almost every night for the past 30 years. As I started my divorce process and began navigating a feeling of loss, I started saying the prayer also in the morning. I want to share it with you.

Dear God, please let your light shine through me—your love, your radiance, and your purity. Help me to be a magnet for you, to bring others close to you, to feel you. I love you, God. I love you, Universe. I am here to serve. Put me where you want me to be. Help me to create peace and harmony. Thank you for teaching me that if I love myself first, then I can love others.

I hope you will find it to be a useful tool as you work to gain strength, hope, and clarity through your transition.

Positive Affirmations

for the Crown Chakra

I am pure love and light.

I am sure of my inner knowing.

I am aware of divine guidance at all times.

I am able to see the big picture.

I seek to understand and to learn from my life experiences.

I look inside myself to discover who I am.

I trust my inner guidance unconditionally.

INTUITION

INNER AWARENESS

PERCEPTION

CLARITY

PURPOSE

WISDOM

STEP 2

CHOOSE THE STORY THAT BELONGS TO YOU

Ajana ❋ Third Eye Chakra

LOCATION: *Brow*

COLOR: *Blue*

STONE: *Lapis*

OIL: *Sandalwood*

SOUND: *OM*

THEME: *Intuition*

HEALING PROPERTY: *Control and Wisdom*

GIFT: *To see the truth, Clarity*

LIFE ISSUE: *Illusion, Unclarity*

ARCHETYPE: *Clairvoyant*

The *Ajana Chakra is all about perception.* It is located between your eyebrows and is directly related to the pineal gland in your brain; it is in charge of sleep, dreams, and intuition. When you need a boost of intuition, call on your third eye. Focusing on this chakra reveals to us an experience of peace, intuition, and inner awareness.

Many start their awareness work with their Ajana Chakra, as it is the easiest chakra to ignite and often helps other chakras to open. Working with your Ajana energy will help you enhance your intuition and gain a clearer view of your purpose in the world.

By focusing on this chakra, you will connect to wisdom, clarity of vision, and increased intuition, allowing you to begin to see life's bigger picture.

Maybe you are searching among the branches
for what appears only in the roots.
—RUMI

AVOIDING THE EMOTIONAL WORK ONLY KEEPS YOU STUCK IN DESPAIR AND SELF-DOUBT

There are many different emotions you experience leading to accepting that your relationship is coming to an end. Pain, being "stuck," clinging, chaos, anxiety, fear, disconnecting, doubt, hurt, ambiguity, and confusion. The partner who is pulling away is struggling with deciding if it is truly bad enough to leave or tolerable enough to stay. The decision between potentially hurting your partner or staying in a relationship pretending to feel something you do not feel is daunting. There is no such thing as a guilt-free option. It seems to me that the best answer comes from honoring the truth.

THE RELATIONSHIP BECOMES MORE DAMAGED WITH AMBIGUITY

The partner wanting to leave the marriage will sometimes become ambivalent about ending the relationship and string their partner along. This causes only more pain and confusion for the other spouse. Although it is not done with malice, it still is quite harmful. Ambiguity brings unnecessary pain to your partner. Although you may not necessarily want the relationship to end immediately, giving your partner false hope will only exaggerate their feelings of resentment and anger. This will eventually lead to a struggle for clarity in the relationship—which will put you both on the defensive.

The partner who wants to leave becomes scared about the hurt they are going to cause their spouse—and, potentially, their children—with the breakup. What the partner who wants to leave doesn't realize is that their partner and children are hurt more when the initiating parent is not fully present—they don't understand where they stand. Ambiguity in a relationship breeds uncertainty and fear. The ambiguity and avoidance cause the partner who wants the relationship to stay intact to feel that there is hope for things to change. The partner withdrawing may become even more aware that they want to leave but doesn't want to say so as a way to avoid causing pain, messiness, and conflict in the relationship.

*I won't be made useless, I won't be idle with despair,
I will gather myself around my faith, for light
is the darkness most feared.*
—JEWEL

If you are the partner who is being left behind, although you may wish for things to be different, you know the truth in your heart. Sometimes the fear of facing our truth is actually worse than the reality of walking in our truth. When you are not authentically loved, and when you know your spouse is no longer committed to the relationship, it is so painful because you feel such a sense of abandonment. There is no hiding it when a relationship is surviving just out of habit or obligation. Initially, you feel shocked when you hear the news. Once you are able to calm the pain, you can start to see the signs that were there all along—the signs that you so desperately tried to avoid.

Many times, when you are the partner being left, it is hard to see the truth, as you are struggling with the pain of feeling abandoned and the pain that comes with no longer being chosen by your partner. You have to ask yourself: "Am I staying because I'm still in love with my partner? Am I staying out of comfort and habit? Am I staying out of fear of the divorce being perceived as a failure?" You deserve to be loved and honored. If your partner can no longer give you that, love yourself enough to separate gracefully, and know that you are a lovely person and that you deserve to be chosen.

The soul has no secret that the behavior
does not reveal.
—LAO TZU

A friend of mine who has been divorced for five years and who now has a wonderful co-parenting relationship with her former husband shared a story from her former husband's perspective. He did not want their marriage to end. He knew that she did, but she had told him that she would explore couples therapy with him. After a painful year, they agreed to divorce. He told her that, in retrospect, he knew that she explored therapy only to assuage her guilt, as she knew that the marriage was over. It almost damaged their future co-parenting relationship, and he was resentful that she strung him along and prolonged the pain. I believe the lesson is: Honor your truth. Do not prolong the pain. If you do, it will only prevent you both from being able to move on. Giving your partner false hope is not good for the future of your relationship, co-parenting or otherwise.

YOU CAN NAVIGATE THROUGH WITH LOVE AND GRACE IF YOU ARE BRAVE AND OWN YOUR TRUTH

Divorce does not need to be based on anger and bitterness. You once loved this person. This person was a gift to you at one time, and you both experienced part of your life's journey together. While their current role in your life may be coming to an end or changing, accept and honor what you once had. Even if they have hurt you or betrayed you, know that carrying angry and vengeful feelings will only hurt you in the end. You will *always* regret getting down in the mud with them. You will *never* regret acting with love and grace. While you cannot control how they behave, you can control how you behave. Remember—it is not the snakebite that kills you; it is the venom that is left behind.

Peace is the result of retraining your mind to process life as it is, rather than as you think it should be.
—WAYNE DYER

During times of transition, your initial reaction may be to fight back, protect yourself, and wallow in "what could have/should have been." The fact is that, if you are in the process of divorce, that dream has already ended or is about to come to an end. That does not mean you need to look at it as a failure, a disappointment, or a sad ending. It is all about perspective. Society has created this vision of "happily ever after," meaning to stay together to the very end. The question I pose is: Is that *truly* "happily ever after"? Can "happily married" be the first fifteen years (or however long you were happily married)? Why does it have to be that if you do not grow old and die together you did not have a happy marriage? How about focusing and viewing it as you were happy for a while, but then that changed—you both grew in different directions, had different priorities, and decided to move on. Focus on the fact that the marriage was not "a failure." It served its purpose for a time, and now, for whatever reason, one or both of you are being called to move on.

How many friends/people do you know who say they are ". . . staying together for the kids"? I'm not sure that the kids are being served, and I can assure you that if you are no longer committed, *you* are not being served. I think many times ". . . the kids . . ." are used as an excuse to stay together, but, in the end, the kids are smarter than you think, and they can see exactly what is going on. They can feel the tension and frustration; perhaps staying together is not the best way to model a healthy relationship for them.

What is the greatest risk? Letting go of what people think—or letting go of how I feel, what I believe, and who I am?"
—BRENE BROWN

Your kids know so much more than they let you know. They know if you're happy or if there are issues. They are able to sense and feel what is going on. In my view, the best thing we can do for our kids is to model healthy relationships. If you are not currently connected and showing your kids what a high-functioning, healthy relationship looks like, they are going to learn only by what they see. Do you want to model an unhealthy situation? So many times kids say, "I wish they would have separated sooner; the tension and hostility between my parents was a lot to handle." The children feel a heaviness when things are strained in their parents' relationship.

Building a strong and healthy self starts with first understanding your truth. Only you know your truth, and only you can help yourself get to your truth. The interesting thing about getting to your truth is that we all have a way of creating our story that is sometimes not as factual as reality. We like to tell ourselves our story in a manner that we are at ease with hearing, but we alter some of the key details because the truth is not something we are willing to accept. We alter our reality for many reasons, such as shame, guilt, embarrassment, disappointment, or plain, old ego needs. I encourage you to tell yourself the real story; only then can you help yourself heal.

You either walk inside your story and own it,
or you stand outside your story and hustle
for your worthiness.
—BRENE BROWN

As the world you knew is shattering around you, the last thing you think about is nurturing yourself. It seems like crazy timing to focus on nurturing yourself when you are merely trying to survive and reduce the collateral damage that is occurring within you and around you. The risk of not taking care of yourself is that you will be coming from a place of being reactive as opposed to being proactive. In order to have a semblance of control over the process, commit to being proactive. Taking care of yourself during this time allows you to think more confidently and creatively so you may see yourself in a more positive light. It is easy to fall into the trap of feeling that we deserve this situation, or that we did something wrong, or that we are not good enough, which leads us to being harsh, unloving, and judgmental toward ourselves and others.

YOUR MIND WILL ALWAYS BELIEVE WHAT YOU TELL IT. NOURISH IT WITH FAITH, NOURISH IT WITH TRUTH, AND NOURISH IT WITH LOVE

The Bhagavad Gita, *a Sanscript scripture says,* "The mind under control is your best friend; the mind wandering about is your worst enemy." You have the power to make your mind your best friend. Your mind is built on the constructs with which you nourish it. Work on aligning your mind with your heart. It is your wise companion that is always trying to protect you. Life's situations often do not change, but the way we choose to perceive situations can change. Choose hope over fear and despair. Transitioning out of marriage will be one of the hardest and scariest things that you will ever experience. Take charge and navigate through your transition with faith and hope. Choose your thoughts so you can choose your experiences. Taking the path of faith and hope will positively serve you, your spouse, and your family. Someone needs to lead with love and grace. Let it be you.

HOW DO WE WORK WITH THE AJANA CHAKRA— THE THIRD EYE—TO GET GROUNDED IN OUR NEW REALITY AND PROCEED WITH GUIDANCE AND LOVE FROM OUR INNER SELF?

The Third-Eye Chakra, intuition, is a great chakra to connect to. The power to navigate through this difficult process with love and grace is in our mind because it opens us to the good around us. A healthy state of mind helps us to expand the realm of new possibilities and to take the focus off of feeling loss. A healthy state of mind lets us see the horizon when we are feeling scared, tired, and confused.

In order to best access your Third-Eye Chakra, focus on affirmations of your goodness and self-worth. When we affirm our goodness, we plant positive thoughts in our subconscious mind. This helps us take the focus off of failure and redirects our vision to include greater potential, possibilities, and hope for emotional happiness and well-being. It is here, with our Third-Eye Chakra, that we begin the healing process and allow ourselves to love and care for ourselves through the transition process. This is empowering, as it is here that we start to see our realm of new possibilities, and we can begin to release our attachment to our former dream.

Remember that what we have seen and heard from other divorces includes only the experiences those individuals choose to have. We can mimic those experiences, or we can write our own stories of what our divorce will look like. Imagine and feel for a moment the difference between these two stories:

Story 1—My marriage failed, and my dream of happiness ever after is lost forever. Of course it failed, because I do not deserve to be happy; it is no surprise this happened. I am not enough; if I were better, prettier, skinnier, kinder, and smarter, this never would have happened to me. I knew this was too good to be true—it was just a matter of time. Now I am living the life of a failed marriage. I cannot stand my ex, and I am going to make him/her miserable through every step of this process.

Story 2—My marriage served me well for the first fifteen years. I have grown from it, and now it is time to move on to my next experience. This is not an ending but rather a new beginning, with infinite possibilities that I have the power to create. I will take all that I have learned, both good and bad, and create the new, loving dream that I deserve. I believe my partner did the best he/she could do, and I hope he/she, too, finds the love and happiness that he/she deserves.

The freedom to choose your story belongs to you. You truly are in control of how you navigate through this divorce process. The truth is that we all have the ability to change the way we look at our lives. If you nourish your mind and nurture yourself, you can create a healthier reality. Your mind can open the door to true healing. You can connect to the power of your mind through yoga and meditation. The benefit of all this is that as the mind becomes healthier, so does the body. When you think positively, you feel a sense of hope. The key is to detach from holding on to negative stories that no longer serve you. The negative stories serve only to savage your well-being, while the positive new stories can open you up to the love and light that is around you.

By connecting to your Third-Eye Chakra, you can also extract wisdom from your past experiences. As you are going through your divorce process, take time to stop and ask yourself what you have learned from this difficult process, what your soon-to-be ex has taught you, and how you will use it to serve you in future relationships. How often do we say to ourselves, "I don't know what to do"? The truth is that the answers to our problems are within us—we just need to get quiet and listen. It is easy to say, "I wish I knew what to do" and then just stay in your vague uncertainty. The reality is that you have the answers—you just need to get quiet and listen to what your heart is telling you. Passive hope is not effective, and it is an excuse to remain stuck and do nothing.

When you're feeling that you need clarity, connect with your Third-Eye chakra to enable you to see and acknowledge your current experience in a truthful manner—not the story you *want to tell* but the *real* story. When you tap into your Third-Eye Chakra, you can understand your experiences and your role in the story, and you can open up to where this new path is taking you.

MY STORY:

My lesson was about boundaries. I think I wanted so much to be loved and to have peace that I set boundaries but did not hold them. I talked a good game, but I was not able to hold my boundaries for fear of causing friction. My pattern was to release my boundary as soon as I sensed that there could be confrontation or that I could be creating waves.

Daring to set boundaries is about having the courage to love ourselves even when we risk disappointing others.
—**BRENE BROWN**

Instead, I would sweep it under the rug and hope that it would go away and that things would get better. Guess what I learned the hard way: it does *not* go away, and the boundaries get more and more compromised over time. One day, I woke up and felt so unfulfilled and discouraged with the situation that I became frustrated and negative. At that point, the boundaries had washed away, and it was too late to repair them. Honoring myself and my boundaries moving forward will serve me well in my future relationships.

I am learning that by setting and holding boundaries, you are not only loving and honoring yourself, you are also telling other loved ones that you love yourself and are setting parameters on what is important for you in the relationship. The reality is that if someone cannot honor that, that behavior is questionable.

Another lesson for me was about having a partner who does not quiet my voice. It is amazing to me how many smart, strong, and intelligent women have their voices quieted by their partners. If this is you, you are not alone. When we look for the answers outside of ourselves, we are not honoring our spirit, and we are closing ourselves off from our inner wisdom. As you tap into your Third-Eye Chakra, intuition, you are better able to access your internal guidance.

I have learned that you cannot run away from the pain associated with divorce. You can stay busy and surrounded by friends and family as much as you want, but, eventually, the need to heal pops up, and you have to deal with it. It is also my belief that in order to bring your "best you" to your new situation, you have to do the work to heal and grow from your past relationship. Owning your story, creating a healthy context for honoring your life experience, forgiving yourself, forgiving the past, looking forward with a positive outlook, and keeping your eye on the light that is ahead are all keys to transitioning with love and grace. In my experience working with women in transition, I often hear them say, "There is so much light at the end." What an interesting term—one that's not often used. But I can vouch for it myself. There truly is so much light at the end of the process if you allow your heart to stay open and loving.

POSITIVE AFFIRMATIONS

Third-Eye Chakra

I choose to release and forgive my past.

This is not an ending but rather a new beginning.

In this situation, there is an opportunity for growth and healing.

I am the source of truth in my life, and I have all the answers I need.

I trust myself and my inner guidance and wisdom.

I trust that I am on the path I am meant to be on.

I am open to all new possibilities, people, places, and experiences.

STEP 3

CONSCIOUS CONVERSATIONS:
SETTING THE COURSE FOR THE FUTURE

Vishuddha ❧ Throat Chakra

LOCATION: *Throat*

COLOR: *Turquoise*

STONE: *Turquoise*

OIL: *Amber Cashmere*

SOUND: *HAM*

THEME: *Communication*

HEALING PROPERTY: *Clearness and Expression*

GIFT: *Making yourself heard*

LIFE ISSUE: *Not honoring y our voice*

ARCHETYPE: *Artisan*

he Throat Chakra rules creativity, communication, and growth. The name of this chakra means "Pure." Focusing on this chakra brings increased mental clarity and the ability to transmit and receive the truth. Your Throat Chakra will help you to speak your truth without fear and help you to understand your life's purpose; it will also help you with expressing yourself and with non-verbal communication.

When you focus on this chakra, it will help you honor your authentic voice and empower you to communicate truth on all levels. Your Throat Chakra is a very powerful doorway to true happiness and freedom.

It has been said that the Vishuddha, the Throat Chakra, is the bridge between your heart and your mind. If the bridge is blocked, impulses are obstructed, and ideas, hopes, and dreams are unable to be realized. If it is unblocked and flowing, you will be able to take responsibility for decisions and speak up for what you want and believe to be the truth. It is also where you develop a spiritual voice and learn to express the truth in your heart and the ideas in your mind.

SETTING THE TONE—THE ENDING CAN BE A POSITIVE BEGINNING

What a terrifying and sad thought to have to tell your spouse you are no longer willing or able to stay in the marriage. This is probably one of the most difficult conversations that you will ever have. It is also one of the most important conversations that you will ever have, because it sets the tone for the huge transition you are both about to embark upon.

This is where you can set the tone for a divorce with love and grace. It is critical to not blame your partner or to make them feel solely responsible. It is equally important not to view the marriage as a failure. It had its time when it did work, and you were both happy. As I questioned at the beginning of this book, why do we consider marriage a failure if you do not stay together until one of you passes away? Why can't we simply honor that the marriage was successful for a period of time and that, now, it simply no longer works? We are all separate beings, and sometimes the path that we're on changes. It is not always going to be the same path for both partners. Sometimes there is a fork in the road and separate paths may need to be taken.

How you end your marriage truly matters. The conversation will set the tone for future experiences for both you and your partner. Often how a relationship ends is how we define the entire relationship. The gentler, kinder, and more understanding the ending is, the more able your spouse will be able to move forward with a positive new beginning. In order for your spouse to take away a positive meaning from your relationship, the ending is just as important as the best memory you have shared together—because the ending is what your spouse ends up remembering. Life challenges, loss, and difficulty can be great teachers if we can view them as learning experiences. There are many lessons that come from the ending of relationships. The breakup can serve as a way to surrender and understand that you cannot control what your partner did, and it helps us learn how to forgive.

So, how do you begin this very difficult conversation? First of all, if you have not done so already, this is a great time to seek some professional advice. If you are not currently working with a therapist or a psychologist, invest in your future now. Girlfriends are an amazing support system, but they are not able to serve in the way that an unbiased professional can. You have a chance to end something that was once precious to both of you. Why not seek advice so that you are well positioned to articulate your thoughts and plans from a place of strength rather than weakness?

The wound is the place where light enters you.
—RUMI

HOW TO SET THE FOUNDATION FOR "A GOOD END"

There are many things that cause the breakdown of a marriage, such as poor communication or the loss of connection. The conversation regarding ending your marriage should not take the same form as your problems. This conversation should ideally come from a place of strength and clear direction. The problem may be that you are most likely currently lacking both. Therefore, seeking outside guidance from a professional will provide you with proven tools that will help you initiate the conversation from a place of kindness. In my opinion, divorce is a form of loss in the sense that the relationship you had will no longer be, and the role of your soon-to-be-former spouse will officially come to an immediate halt once you have your conversation.

I don't know that love changes. People change. Circumstances change.
—NICHOLAS SPARKS

So, the interesting thing is that it is all about perspective. You can decide to label it a "bad marriage" and say that your partner was impossible and that it is no wonder that the marriage failed. Or you could look at the same situation through a completely different lens and say it was "a very successful marriage for many years." There was love, compassion, caring, passion, and good parenting, but over the last couple of years, you and your spouse have grown apart. You still care about each other and are committed to co-parenting and having the children feel supported and loved by their parents.

Ending a relationship can be done in a manner that preserves the dignity of both partners. If done with love and grace, it can mitigate the feelings of pain and loss. Remember always that you both once truly cared for each other and that you owe it to each other to have an open and honest conversation about why the marriage unraveled. Whether you are the partner who is choosing to leave or the partner who is being left, you both need to honor what was and what happened and share it in a kind and caring way. The greatest issues people have with breakups is the lack of understanding about what occurred and the resulting lack of closure.

BE BRAVE, BE REAL, AND BE VULNERABLE

A healthy conversation about ending a marriage takes a great deal of maturity, courage, and the ability to be vulnerable and real. Before initiating the conversation, think clearly, and reflect deeply on why you think you need to end the marriage if you are the one initiating the discussion. There needs to be some planning and thoughtfulness around the discussion. What are the issues that led to this decision? Have you grown apart? Are there habits and values your spouse has that do not align with yours? Here is an interesting thing to consider: what we love in others, we love in ourselves; what we dislike in others is what we do not like about ourselves. This is a good time to truly connect with self and be real and honest about how you have arrived at this place. Once you can articulate to *yourself* why you need to leave the marriage, it will be easier for you to have a meaningful discussion with your partner.

At the start and at the end of a relationship, true intimacy is a risky business. It takes a lot of strength to show up and be real. Love is something we constantly need to nurture and grow. When we reach barriers that prevent us from being able to grow our relationship, we start to feel emptiness and hopelessness.

Live your life with love and bravery
and you shall lead a life uncommon.
—JEWEL

If there are children involved, these conversations are even more heart-wrenching. Again, how you present it to the children is critical. You have known about the impending divorce for much longer and have had your time to process it. This is most likely going to be a surprise to them. Help them understand that the marriage no longer works but that the family will always work. It is important to have the entire family gathered together and to be kind and respectful with each other. The children need as much strength and stability as possible during this difficult conversation.

How do we make divorce easier for our children? Children want to understand, first and foremost, how this is going to affect their lives. It is important to have a plan in place with some clarity as to how their time will be divided between the parents, where they will be living with each parent, and what their school situation will be. It is important to emphasize that the greatest change for them is that they will be going from one loving household to two loving households.

Divorce isn't such a tragedy. A tragedy is staying in an unhappy marriage, teaching your children the wrong things about love.
—JENNIFER WEINER

As angry, hurt, and disappointed as you may be with your spouse, adult issues should remain as such. The children should never be exposed to adult issues.

If you choose to say something negative about their other parent, you are creating distance in your child's relationship with that parent and, potentially, slowly tearing it apart. Your child will also have more difficulty in navigating through the transition.

You and your spouse may have decided to part ways, but the children should feel comfortable and free to love both parents, with no need to ever choose between them. It is critical to their success in navigating through the transition that they are not caught in the middle—they don't need to hear either parent speaking negatively of the other parent. They definitely do not need to know about the details that led to the divorce. Most of the research that I read indicates that divorce is not what hurts the children. The children get hurt and potentially damaged for life when the parents speak negatively of one another and make the divorce a very negative and volatile situation for the children. Think about it: both parents are part of those children, and, if you insult the other parent, you are insulting the children and putting them in an uncomfortable situation.

The greatest gift you can give your children is a calm and peaceful relationship with their other parent. It is particularly important that you validate their memories and feelings about the past. One of my clients told me that she keeps family pictures up with her ex-husband in them. Her reason for doing this is to let her children know that there were good times and that she still honors those happy memories as an important part of their family history.

WHAT WILL YOUR PR (PUBLIC RELATIONS) STORY BE? LESS IS BEST

The beauty of divorcing with love and grace is that you are setting the stage for a more calm and peaceful future for your children and for each other. In my opinion, it is key to honor your partner/spouse and children during this process by keeping personal details about the divorce *private*. When I was going through my divorce, I had a very meaningful conversation with my soon-to-be-ex-husband. I told him that I thought we needed to have a consistent PR story that we could share with casual friends, acquaintances, and co-workers. Way too many times, people announcing their divorce do so in a such a way that they appear to be trying to make a case for being the innocent one in the divorce. To me, that is ego, and I did not want either of us pleading our case at the risk of hurting each other and our family.

I suggested we both have the same PR statement and simply say, "Our marriage was a happy marriage for a long time. Over the last couple of years, we have grown apart and changed. It is no one's fault, and we both agree, although the marriage no longer works, that we love our kids more than anything and that the *family* will always work." Our PR statement was short, and it was truthful, but, more importantly, it kept our private situation private and protected our children. The common response was, "But you always looked so happy, and I thought you had it all—the perfect couple and family." We would answer, "We *were* happy for a long period of time. We have just grown apart and have decided that we would be better off separate; we agreed to be committed to co-parenting together."

The sad reality is that there are many couples who are not happy but who are choosing to stay together by default. They cannot or don't want to face their reality. It is interesting how some of these individuals connected with me as I was going through the divorce process. I think that, in some strange way, my situation empowered them with the ability to face their reality and realize that they are not alone in what they are experiencing. Whether they acted on it or not, I gave them permission to accept that what they were feeling is okay. If they were not close friends, I was always cautious with what I would share. I would also always encourage everyone to do whatever they could to work on their marriage first. Divorce should always be a last resort.

On the flip side, it was interesting to see how happily married friends would respond. I would say that announcing your divorce to friends, whether they are happily married or not, always feels like the moment of truth. It is the time that you learn who is there for you and who may not be willing to engage in the same manner after the divorce. I must say I was lucky, as I was quite pleasantly surprised. I often wonder if that has anything to do with our PR story and the fact that I was committed to having love and grace be my mantra through my process. I believe that we should regard our friends, family, and colleagues in the same way that we do our children: they do not want to be dragged through the anger and bitterness that comes from divorce. In their own way, they are experiencing their own changes due to the divorce.

I remember getting a call from the former PTO president of my children's elementary school. This woman was all about kids and family, and I thought I was going to take my first official hit. I thought she was going to confront me about

"How could you do this to your husband and kids by wanting to get divorced?" I was bracing myself for the smack-down. Instead, after our call, I still wanted to cry—but for a whole different reason. She was calling to tell me how much she admired and respected me for how I worked full-time as a financial advisor yet always volunteered for everything and was always present for my children at school and at their sports. She said she knew I didn't have much support, as my parents had passed away. She wanted me to know that she would be there if I ever needed coverage with the kids. She almost brought me to my knees—it was just the kindest, most-caring outreach I had ever received. She ended the call by telling me she was surprised about how we'd managed to deliver this news to our community in a way that had no one talking about us. The gossip mill was kept at bay. I think a lot of it had to do with our consistent PR message and honoring each other and our privacy. I think the rest of it was that we were not sharing any negative stories about each other. We were both attending our kids' events, sitting together, and being cordial and kind with each other.

HOW TO SET THE TONE FOR FRIENDS— INVITES TO EVENTS

The "PR story" has ramifications also for getting invited to events/gatherings and how to handle that. As we were in the midst of starting our divorce, there was a graduation party for our friend's daughter. The wife called me up and invited me to the party, saying, "We want you to know that we are on your side and will not be inviting your soon-to-be-ex-husband, if that makes you feel more comfortable." I immediately said, "Thank you so much. I know you are coming from a loving place, but the truth is that there are no 'sides' in our situation. We are getting divorced, but that does not mean we are dividing up our friendship pool." I let her know that both she and her husband meant a lot to us and that we both wanted them in our lives. In addition, I told her I never wanted them to feel that they had to choose sides. I suggested they treat us as they always had and encouraged her to feel comfortable inviting both of us. Your friends should not have to choose. You should be adult enough to attend gatherings together and be respectful and cordial. I guaranteed her that, if one of us was uncomfortable, we would respectfully decline and that we would never put our friends in the middle of who they choose to invite to a gathering.

It is important for the healing process that you avoid creating negative situations whenever possible. Although it is not always easy, it is beneficial for your well-being and for others involved. You should have your inner circle that you can share all the good, bad, and ugly information with, and this would include your therapist. You will need a safe place where you can be authentic and vulnerable. My advice to you is choose wisely who you let into your real world. They can be the lifeline you need to stay above water or they can be the undertow that causes you to work harder to stay above water.

HOW DO WE USE THE THROAT CHAKRA TO COMMUNICATE EFFECTIVELY?

The Throat Chakra is in charge of communication. If you effectively tap into your Throat Chakra, it guides you and helps you speak the truth without fear; it connects you with expressing your life's purpose. When you focus on the Throat Chakra, you will be supported in speaking your truth. The Throat Chakra opens up the way for true freedom and happiness, because you are using your voice to honor yourself. When your Throat Chakra is aligned, you can be genuine and share your soul's path in a loving and authentic way.

When we are navigating through divorce, the Throat Chakra can easily shut down from feeling anger, fear, and grief. It becomes compromised when we are not speaking our truth. When you first start to express your intention to divorce to your spouse, children, family, friends, and coworkers, it is imperative that you honor your truth so that your Throat Chakra does not become compromised. In order to maintain a sense of honoring yourself, it is essential that you express your truth as clearly as you can, even at the risk of being different or stepping outside of what is the perceived norm among your tribe. A very good friend of mine, Dr. Dorothy Martin Neville, wrote a book entitled *Real Women Change the World: Letting the Good Girl Die So the Real Woman Can Live.* Dr. Dorothy is a successful psychologist and author. She has kindly and sometimes not-so-kindly reminded me that I need to stop trying to always be "the good girl" and learn to honor what I need. Thank goodness for Dorothy. Whatever your story is, honor it, express it, and own it. If you feel you've made bad choices, own it. Step into your truth, and then let it go.

Growth is painful; change is painful.
But nothing is as painful as staying stuck
somewhere you don't belong.

When you are contemplating divorce or facing the fact that you are not happy but find yourself quieting your voice, this is normally an indicator that change is needed. Saying "No" to situations or relationships that may be empty or even harmful is essential to honoring ourselves and nurturing a strong will. When you suppress your emotions, it stops energy from flowing, and it also keeps you from knowing your inner truth. When you begin to own your truth, you begin to heal and open the Throat Chakra. Almost all negative experiences are suppressed in the throat. The reason this happens is that you fail to acknowledge what you feel, no matter how hurt or angry you may be. The expression *"The truth will set you free"* is beyond wise. Although it may be difficult to get the words out at times, once they are out, you feel a sense of relief and peace.

The Throat Chakra also oversees your ears. You can reinforce this chakra when you hear and honor your inner voice. When you listen quietly to self, you open the door to your Throat Chakra. This is difficult, yet necessary, to do as you set your path on your divorce journey. This may be one of the biggest challenges you will face with yourself. Be brave enough to face your feelings and accept them for what they are. The key is to communicate them during the divorce process in a kind and graceful way. When you are able to tell the truth about how you're feeling, you empower yourself to take a deeper look at your reality.

MY STORY

I struggled for more than six years to hear my truth. I tried hard to quiet my voice and to do everything I could to hold it all together. In retrospect, the reasons I was trying to hold it all together were ego-based, not heart-based. I was worried about what people would think and how I would navigate as a divorced woman. I didn't want to feel as if I had failed. I thought that if I just did more, I could change my circumstances, and I could get him to change.

The truth began to come out slowly, during girls' nights after a couple of glasses of wine. It started off with questions such as, "Is it normal when . . ." Invariably, soon after sharing stories, I'd see a look of disappointment on my friends' faces. On the surface, we looked like a happy couple with a beautiful family. The reality was that there was a huge disconnect and a feeling of loneliness and helplessness. I remember waking up in the middle of the night, thinking, *How did I get so disconnected from this person? I feel like I don't even know my husband anymore.*

When a beautiful, young, and vivacious 70-year-old friend of mine started sharing about her current relationship, it sounded amazing. She shared about their strong physical connection but also about their deep communication. When I shared that I had lost a sense of communication, she said, "You've allowed your voice to be quieted." I was shocked to hear that, and my immediate response was going to be "No, that's not true." But, suddenly, it hit me. It was true. I got the boulder through my windshield. How could I be such a strong woman but allow my voice to be quieted? It didn't make sense. But, in reality, when I got quiet and connected with self, it was the truth.

POSITIVE AFFIRMATIONS

for the Throat Chakra

*Expressing my voice and hearing my truth is vital
to my well-being.*

I express my truth as kindly and lovingly as possible.

I trust the guidance from my inner voice, and I hear the truth.

*I listen to the truth that others share, and I share my truth
openly and honestly.*

I am open to speaking my truth without judgment.

I honor myself enough to know that my truth is my compass.

*I know that the deepest and truest connections are built
on sharing our truths.*

STEP 4

UNWIND YOUR MARRIAGE WITH LOVE AND GRACE

Anahatha ❀ Heart Chakra

LOCATION: *Heart*

COLOR: *Green*

STONE: *Rose quartz*

OIL: *Rose*

SOUND: *YAM*

THEME: *Soul's Intention*

HEALING PROPERTY: *Self-acceptance*

GIFT: *To love and be loved*

LIFE ISSUE: *Sorrow*

ARCHETYPE: *Healer*

he Heart Chakra is located at the center of your chest. This energy point is all about transformation, love, beauty, compassion, and empathy. It allows you to connect deeply. Focus on this chakra when you need to see love and feel love and when you need the strength to create and support the heart's desires. The Sanskrit word *anahatha* translates literally as "un-stuck." The Heart Chakra also radiates your soul's intention and feelings, making this a powerful place of manifestation.

When you are going through divorce, both you and your partner may be stuck in a cycle of pain. You will have different stories as to how the marriage got to this point, yet you will be experiencing similar degrees of pain. Ending a marriage is one of the most painful processes to transition through. Ruin is a gift. Ruin is the road to transformation. The only way out is love. The heart thrives on joy, kindness, sharing, connection, and touch. However, it closes with pain, trauma, and loss. Although you may no longer be in each other's lives the way you used to be, you can still choose to love your soon-to-be-ex in a new way and honor them for the life and the lessons shared.

New beginnings are often disguised
as painful endings.
—Lao Tzu

I know it sounds hard to believe, but you truly can choose love. You do not have to share the same traumatic divorce experience that you have witnessed among friends, your co-workers, or your parents. You have the power to create your own loving journey. I'm sure you are thinking, *You do not know my partner.* I don't, but I do know that while you cannot control how *they* choose to navigate the divorce process, you *can* choose how *you* approach the situation. That's not to say there will not be times when you break, and do or say something out of character. As hard as I try, I have had my moments. But I've learned that I *always* regret when I do not come from a place of love and grace, and I *never* regret not reacting to a situation in a negative matter. If you choose to focus on getting back to love, your heart will heal much faster, and you will navigate through this process with less collateral damage to you, your spouse, and your children.

You have the power to heal your life, and you need to know that. We think so often that we are helpless, but we're not. We always have the power of our minds... Claim and consciously use your power.
—Louise Hay

So, what tools do you use to keep love in your heart? The first step is to release blame, old stories, old pain, and the feeling that the marriage was a failure. Open up to surrendering to the universe and letting go of the perception that the entire marriage was a failure and that you do not like this person. Open up to the goodness and love you once shared. Understand that there is no right or wrong. People come into your lives for a reason—usually to teach you a lesson—but they are not always intended to stay forever. Staying forever does not necessarily constitute a successful marriage.

The second step is to forgive yourself. If you are feeling guilty because you are the one who has decided to end the marriage, make peace with yourself. Stop waiting for your ex to forgive you. Forgive yourself. Forgive yourself for letting go; forgive yourself for hanging on too long. Forgiveness is the biggest lesson in this journey. If you do not learn to forgive yourself, you will hurt yourself. If you are the spouse who is being left, don't spend any time blaming your partner for wanting to leave or blaming yourself for causing the breakup of the marriage. Nothing will be gained.

Your partner may be enhancing the feeling of guilt by reminding you constantly that you are responsible for ending the marriage. Think logically: if you were happy and fulfilled, ending the marriage would not be a consideration. As long as you have done all that you can to try to salvage the marriage, move forward with trust and faith that you are following your soul's path and honoring what you need to do for yourself. The reality is that if you stay in a marriage that no longer serves you, then you are betraying your soul.

You may feel that by honoring your soul you are betraying your partner by leaving. Another way to look at this is: are you really doing your partner a favor if you are not choosing them and loving them the way they deserve to be honored and loved? Maybe there is someone else out there who will love and honor them the way they deserve. My belief is that you are not doing anyone any favors by staying if you are no longer choosing your partner.

Moving on doesn't mean forgetting.
It means you choose happiness over hurt.

If your partner is the one who has decided to end the marriage, you might be the one dealing with anger, betrayal, and resentment. How do you make peace with the situation? A powerful way to make peace is to surrender to acceptance. Accept the situation, and make a conscious decision to surrender to the situation. Struggling with it will not change the fact that your partner has made a decision to leave. A Jewel lyric says, *"Nature has a funny way of breaking what does not bend."* Back to our nature analogy: if you observe trees during a storm, the branches that remain rigid and do not bend often break off. The branches that move with the wind and sway back and forth remain intact. Learn to trust in the universe, and surrender to the fact that this, too, shall pass and that you will be okay. In fact, you most probably will be better than okay if you learn to trust. What looks like a dark patch can be a beautiful turning point if you trust the process.

The reality is that you have two choices when navigating through your divorce, and they are fear or hope. If you choose fear, you will allow in uncertainty, insecurity, and limited fulfillment; you will have low expectations for a positive outcome. If you choose hope, you will have a sense of awakening and a strong sense of self, and you will be open to setting your intentions for the outcome that you want. The only way to heal is to have trust and hope. When you focus on helping and honoring yourself, you help all the people you love.

Love is not something we give or get; it is something we nurture and grow, a connection that can only be cultivated between two people when it exists within each of them. We can only love others as much as we love ourselves.

—BRENE BROWN

As you navigate through the process, fall in love with yourself. Give yourself true, pure, unconditional love. Set your intentions for love, radiance, clarity, strength, and peace. If your heart does not like what is going on out there, change what is going on inside. The best way to learn about yourself is through relationships, starting with the relationship with yourself. Balance is about not letting anyone love you less than you love yourself.

HOW DO WE WORK WITH THE HEART CHAKRA TO GET THROUGH OUR DIVORCE WITH LOVE AND GRACE?

Love is something that stays in your heart forever. The qualities of the Heart Chakra are love, peace, joy, innocence, and purity. The Heart Chakra expands and grows through deep connections sharing, touching, and openness. The Heart Chakra closes with loss, pain, and trauma.

The Heart Chakra is made up of two mechanisms. The heart protector is the double wall around the heart, which works to protect the heart from hurt. It works to keep negativity, criticism, and unkind intentions away from the kindness and purity of the heart. We are able to build our protection by developing unconditional love for self. We accomplish this by nourishing our hearts with self-love, healthy boundaries, listening to and following our soul, and quieting our minds. By loving ourselves, our lives, and others, we are sharing a positive light to heal the world.

THE RICHNESS OF DIVORCE

The second mechanism of the Heart Chakra is the actual heart itself. The heart itself is kind, loving, pure, and innocent. We can only count on ourselves to connect to our heart. If we try to find the connection outside ourselves, we will find ourselves back at the starting line of our search.

In the end, only kindness matters.
—JEWEL

The heart suffers when we are going through separation, rejection, or isolation. For our heart to heal, we must forgive, be open, and release old wounds. We must incorporate meditation, stillness, prayer, and acceptance. Peace and fulfillment come from being connected to kindness, love, and forgiveness. Nurture the heart by remaining connected to self, getting quiet, and honoring yourself. Spend time in nature—we can learn much from what we observe. The ultimate key is learning not to look through your head. Look through your heart.

MY STORY

Since I was sixteen, I was either with a boyfriend or breaking up with a boyfriend. I always had someone in my life.

Part of it is that I love being in love. My heart is full of love, and I thrive when I am sharing my love. I was taught at a very young age by my loving grandmother to always choose myself first. She taught me that I needed to love myself unconditionally to be able to love someone else. My grandmother would always reiterate how wonderful I was and she made me feel that I was enough. My grandmother always stressed that, if someone was not honoring or treating me well, I should communicate that. If the person chose not to honor what I needed, it was my responsibility to myself to honor what I needed.

POSITIVE AFFIRMATIONS

for the Heart Chakra

I am love, I am peace, and I am kindness.

Through stillness, I can clearly hear my heart guide me.

Love heals me.

I ground my heart in truth, love, and kindness.

I choose peace in the midst of chaos.

My heart is made up of love and peace.

Regardless of what is happening, I have the power to choose love.

POWER · CONFIDENCE · ESSENCE · WISDOM · BELIEF · AUTHENTIC SELF

STEP 5

COMMIT TO HELPING YOUR CHILDREN THRIVE

Manipura ❧ Solar Plexus Chakra

LOCATION: *Navel*

COLOR: *Yellow*

STONE: *Citrine*

OIL: *Jasmine*

SOUND: *RAM*

THEME: *Power*

HEALING PROPERTY: *Instinctual knowing, Energy*

GIFT: *Authenticity*

LIFE ISSUE: *Self Esteem*

ARCHETYPE: *Champion*

The Solar Plexus Chakra is the power and wisdom chakra. You will benefit by tapping into this chakra when telling the children the news about the divorce, as this chakra holds the key to confidence, personality, opinions, power, and beliefs. It is located at the navel. Focus on this chakra when you need to access your instinct and ignite your essence.

Children want to understand how the divorce is going to affect their lives. As you are formulating how you will break the news to them, put yourself in their place, and try to understand their perspective. Their life is about to change drastically, and they have no control over the changes occurring. This is why it is imperative that you have a plan when you share with them the news about the divorce and clearly define how this will affect them.

When telling the children, it is important to distinguish between the marriage and the family. Be clear that the marriage no longer works but that the family will always work. You and your soon-to-be-ex are choosing to no longer engage as husband and wife, but you will always engage as mom and dad, regardless of the divorce. It is so important for their well-being that they understand that you are both committed to co-parenting and being there for them. The only major change for them maybe that they will be going from one loving household to two loving households.

Next, share your plan for them with mom and dad after the divorce. This will help to ease their anxiety. Reinforce that you are both committed to making the transition peaceful, predictable, and as seamless as possible for them. They will need you to proceed with strength and consistency, as they are relying on both of their parents to lead and support them through this process.

The more details you can share with your children, the more secure they will feel. The children really want to understand how this change that they have no control over is going to affect their lives. For example, the plan could be for mom to remain in the house, while dad moves one mile away. The children will remain in the same school, with the same activities, and with the same friends. The change will be that they will be with dad every Monday and Tuesday and mom every Wednesday and Thursday. Weekends will include Friday, Saturday, and Sunday, and mom and dad will rotate every weekend. See how this amount of detail will bring clarity to understanding how their life will be impacted.

You can raise healthy and resilient children. It's never the divorce that damages the children—it's how the parents treat each other during and after the divorce. If you treat each other with kindness and respect, the children will get through the process with less trauma and damage, and you can actually raise resilient, happy, and secure kids. Remember, they love you both and do not need to be put in the middle of adult issues or be made to feel that they need to choose sides. They truly want to love you both and proceed with their lives without much negative impact.

For the benefit of the children, do not share adult issues with them. They don't need to know the reasons for the divorce. They don't need to know about your negative feelings for their other parent. It is the most damaging thing you can do to your children. Work through your pain with love and grace, and don't drag your children through any of your hurt and resentment. The children do not need to take sides or know negative things about the other parent. If it is the one thing you do well through this process, hold a high standard for how you behave.

A decent person does not alienate children from a parent, no matter how angry they are at the person for the divorce. It's unfair to the children, and it's unfair to your partner.

If you are the partner who is choosing to leave, do not allow yourself to be held captive by your spouse. Many times, your spouse will try to make you feel guilty for breaking up the family. The reality is that you are not leaving the family—you are ending the marriage. Your partner may try to make you feel guilty because they feel scared; they may be experiencing a sense of failure or simply acting from ego. Other times, there is a resistance to the change in lifestyle that will occur as a result of the divorce. You will need to be strong and consistent in order to lead your family through this difficult process. Lingering and waffling will only prolong the pain, and you will lose respect and credibility.

If you are the spouse who is being left, put your own fears and hurt aside, and be strong and unwavering for your children. Do not share your hurt or disappointment over the situation with your children. Especially, do not share any of the adult issues. This is a time to step up and act from love and grace. Even though you may be feeling abandoned, please do not make your children feel as if they are being abandoned. Do not try to "win them over" by sharing negative things about their other parent. Do not put the children in the middle. This is an act that will damage your children for life. Your children can thrive through the divorce process if you both act like mature, respectful, kind, and loving adults. The children will mirror what they see. Please do not allow your insecurities to affect your children. Show them strength, kindness, love, and respectful behavior.

I strongly believe children can thrive through divorce.
Children need parents who love them. Children need
to know they are safe. Children need stability,
and sometimes that's much easier to achieve
outside a marriage than in a broken one.
—UNKNOWN

Your children may be angry, scared, disappointed, and hurt. Honor their process, but know that, in time, this, too, shall pass. If you both are navigating the process respectfully and are not throwing each other under the bus, the kids will heal faster. It is never your responsibility to tell your child negative things about their other parent. They will only grow to resent you in the future. Let them observe and formulate their own decisions. It may take time, but this is *their* truth they need to come to terms with. Let them learn how to have a relationship with each of you in their own way.

Another important thing to consider when discussing the divorce with the children is directing them on how they can communicate the current situation with friends, teachers, and family. I think it is important to honor their process and give them full discretion to tell whomever they feel they would like to reach out to. Encourage them to follow their instincts and to share the current family situation with those in whom they can confide or with whom they simply want to share. Your concern should be that, if they feel they need to keep this a secret, it may bring shame and a feeling of having to hide family secrets. It is critical to helping them accept the situation to display no sense of judgment or embarrassment regarding the divorce. If you can encourage them to just *be* with the current situation, that will bring them confidence and support in going through this huge family-dynamic change.

Sometimes parents ask children not to share the divorce. I strongly believe this is hurtful to the children. Allow them to have their voice. They will feel much safer if they know that they can communicate their feelings about this painful and scary transition and that there is nothing to hide.

You may want to consider sharing with the children a version of the "PR Story" you and your soon-to-be ex have agreed to share with your friends, colleagues, and family. This helps keep everything consistent and under the radar with the gossip crew. It is important for the children to understand the distinction between what is appropriate to share and what should remain private. This is a fine line, as you ultimately want them to feel comfortable sharing their story, their real story, as they see it.

It is equally as important that you fill your own cup during this draining process. You will need to be able to fill the children's cups and cannot do so unless your cup is full. Nurture and give yourself what you need so that you can bring your best self when you are spending time with your children. In order for them to feel positive and happy, they need to be getting positive and happy energy from you. I believe that if we are vibrating on a higher level, the kids will also. They will feed off your energy and your spouse's energy, so do your best to fill your cup so you will have positive energy.

Forgive yourself during this process, and release your feelings of guilt connected to disappointing your children. If the marriage was not working, trust me—the children sense it. The children learn by what they see and not so much by what we say. If they see a disconnected, unhappy couple with little affection or caring for each other, they may model this in their own relationships. They may feel that this is the norm. If you want your children to have loving, connected, caring relationships, it is essential that you show them what that looks like. Don't downplay the importance of honoring yourself and your needs.

Don't judge or place labels on the divorce. If you place labels on it, your children will, too. Labeling and judging tend to lead to a negative path, one that the mind/ego creates out of constructs. As examples: "Of course, the marriage did not work." "I am not worthy of love." "Who could love me unconditionally?" "Of course, my spouse fell out of love with me." All this negative self-talk leads to the most dreadful self-judgment of all: "I am not enough."

The truth is, you *are* enough. Acceptance of what *is* and allowing yourself to surrender is important while navigating through the process.

Focus on being the silent observer. Flow with the situation without placing any labels on it. Surrender to what is, open up, and have faith that this will lead you and your children to the path you are supposed to be on.

FROM THE CHILD'S PERSPECTIVE— QUOTES FROM CHILDREN WHO HAVE EXPERIENCED DIVORCE

Parents shouldn't stay together if they are not in love. (11-year-old girl)

It is better going home to silence than to fighting. Their divorce is better for our family. (12-year-old girl)

It would have been better if my parents had divorced years ago. The fighting and tension were awful. (16-year-old boy)

It's going to be better in the end. (14-year-old boy)

My parents always seemed so tense and unhappy when they were together. It is nice to not feel that anymore; it was not fun to come home to. (15-year-old girl)

HOW TO WORK WITH THE SOLAR PLEXUS CHAKRA TO STAY STRONG AND FOCUSED WHEN TELLING KIDS ABOUT THE DIVORCE

The underlying theme of the Solar Plexus Chakra is self-worth. When connecting with our Solar Plexus Chakra, we create awareness of our worth, esteem, and our true power. Stay grounded when telling your children so that you come from a place of self-worth and power—they will navigate through this process with the same outlook. When you are connected with self, you radiate light and vibrate on a higher level. This is where you want to be when communicating with your children.

This sense of self and power will help you navigate and bring your children through the divorce process. This power can be expressed in any discussion you have with your children. It helps guide you through the challenges and obstacles that are placed in your path during the divorce process and helps with the interactions you have with your children. Without challenges, our "inner grit" and personal power cannot be developed. Once you get through this process, honor yourself and your ability to be connected with your strength. Honor yourself for having the strength and courage to live your truth.

Confidence, self-worth, and acceptance come from experiencing who you really are. Personal power is the ability to lead others and having the tenacity to make difficult changes. You are able to make powerful decisions for yourself and your loved ones when you know your self-worth. When you act from a place of strength and take on a strong role in navigating your destiny, you gain the confidence and trust from your children and make the divorce process easier for them to navigate through.

MY STORY

Telling my children was one of the hardest things I ever had to do. I will never forget the look on their faces. I remember feeling a rush of freezing and paralyzing air go through my body. My ex and I told them together, and, with great guidance from our mediator, we were both very strong and consistent in our delivery. While we had our own challenges at the time, I am proud and grateful that we both put our children first and delivered the news with love and grace.

POSITIVE AFFIRMATIONS

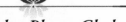

for the Solar Plexus Chakra

I am worthy of creating the life that I want for me and my children.

I have the power to create a happy, fulfilled, and abundant life.

I am worthy of obtaining the life I want.

I am open to all possibilities and am deserving of love, health, and joy.

I choose to bring in goodness, light, and love to my life.

I make the best choices for myself and my loved ones.

I honor myself enough to make the changes I need in order to lead a fulfilled life.

SELF

TRUST

SENSUALITY

ENJOYMENT

CREATIVITY

EMOTIONS

STEP 6

BREAKING OLD PATTERNS AND CREATING NEW PATHS

Svadhisthana ❋ Sacral Chakra

LOCATION: *Abdomen*

COLOR: *Orange*

STONE: *Carnelian*

OIL: *Musk*

SOUND: *VAM*

THEME: *Self*

HEALING PROPERTY: *Pleasure seeking*

GIFT: *To feel pleasure*

LIFE ISSUE: *Guilt*

ARCHETYPE: *Lover*

The *Sacral Chakra is considered* the "dwelling place of self," and it is the foundation for our physical health and overall well-being. It controls our movement and our emotions. It is said to be ruled by the water element, which is directly influenced by how we process our feelings and emotions.

When you hold back your feelings, water is retained, and you feel bloated and puffy. Finding the balance between control and the ability to let go is critical for this chakra to work well. Focus on this chakra so that you may be open to experiencing pleasure, creativity, and balance in your emotions.

Letting go of a situation that no longer serves you is not being heartless and cruel. It means you are choosing yourself. You deserve to be happy, and so does your ex. As long as you have both tried all that you could, you now need to set yourself free and focus on loving and honoring yourself.

The first step is to fall in love with yourself every day. When you look in the mirror, really love and appreciate that person you see. Honor and have compassion for the person who has just overcome so much and is still standing. It is through hardship and loss that you can truly experience self-awareness. The beauty of self-awareness is that it provides us with direct knowledge of self. This is the true gift you receive once you have done the work.

When I let go of what I am, I become what I might be.
When I let go of what I have, I receive what I need.
—LAO TZU

The true foundation for loving yourself starts with liking yourself and accepting yourself exactly as you are, letting go of judgment, which, as we discussed in the previous chapter, leads to labeling, which ultimately leads to "I am not enough." It is helpful to think about treating yourself just as you would treat a friend. You would not constantly point out every negative attribute in a friend—if you did, you would no longer have that friendship.

One day I was on a run and kept playing over and over in my head an event that had occurred that day, judging how I handled it. Then I thought, *If I had a friend speaking to me the way I am speaking to myself, I would no longer want to be their friend.* Talk to yourself with the same love, grace, and compassion with which you would speak to a friend.

You may feel at times that you are not deserving of love, grace, or compassion because you may not operate efficiently if you let the bar down. It is actually quite the opposite: the more you allow yourself a safe and loving place to grow, the better you will become, and the faster you will step into your new self. Also, without practicing love, grace, and compassion for yourself, it is very difficult to bring it to your other relationships. The way you treat yourself is how you will treat others.

The second step in reclaiming your power is to understand how you lost your power/ yourself in your former relationship. The reality is that, for every selfish, self-centered, narcissistic man, there is a woman who lost herself giving him everything she thought he needed in return for his love. On the other side, for every judgmental and demanding woman, there is an insecure man losing himself to try to gain her approval. The focus here is to identify your pattern so that you do not repeat it in your next relationship.

The best way to reclaim your power is to take time to be quiet and still after your transition. Your initial instinct may be to want to stay busy and fill your life with people and activities. By doing so, you will ultimately prolong the healing process. Get quiet and seek awareness; ask yourself how you have given your power away and why. Why have you chosen not to honor yourself? Why have you turned away from the truth or compromised what you need? Why are you afraid of not being loved? Once you give yourself permission, without judgment, to see the unconscious ways you have been participating in relationships by compromising self, you will gain the ability to make different choices in your next relationship. Awareness is the beginning of reclaiming your power.

QUESTIONS THAT CAN HELP BRING AWARENESS:

"Why was I unwilling to honor myself and set/hold boundaries in my relationship?"

"What were the stories I was telling myself to stay in my unhealthy relationship?"

"How did it serve me to choose someone emotionally unavailable in my relationship?"

"Even though promises and commitments were often broken, why did I choose to flow with it and not honor my needs?"

"Did I let myself down in ways similar to how my partner let me down?"

"Why do I feel I will not be loved if I ask for what I need?"

Once you can begin to see and accept things as they really are, without judgment but rather with love, grace, and compassion for yourself, your life can begin to change for the best. This is where the richness of divorce can start to serve you. This is where the ending of the marriage can bring much light and love for you. It is in adversity and loss that we can truly find the beauty of who we are if we allow ourselves to do the work and grow from the experience.

Forgive others, not because they deserve forgiveness,
but because you deserve peace.
—JONATHAN LOCKWOOD HUIE

The final step in loving and honoring yourself is forgiveness. "Forgiving is a gift to yourself. It frees you from the past, past experiences, and past relationships. It allows you to live in the present time. When you forgive yourself and forgive others, you are indeed free." (Louise Hays) The most important aspect to understand about forgiveness is to remember that forgiveness will not change your *past*—it will change your *future*. You are benefiting not only your former partner by forgiving—*you* are the true recipient of forgiveness, for it is where you will find peace and freedom.

The person who is the hardest to forgive is the one
who can teach you the greatest lessons. When you
love yourself enough to rise above the old situations,
then understanding and forgiveness will be easy.
And you will be set free.
—**Louise Hay**

I have often heard that it takes an entire year after the divorce is final to feel somewhat normal. Having lived through it, I can tell you that there is a lot of truth behind that. It is a process of experiencing the seasons and holidays for the first time in your new paradigm. It is a process to get used to your new daily routine and to learn how to bring new, fulfilling things into your life. You will find emotions rising and energy sometimes being drained. Give yourself time to be quiet and still. This will allow you to build your new life from a proactive rather than reactive place.

There is no way around it: divorce or ending a relationship brings with it some collateral damage. The vulnerability and lessons learned can be part of the beauty you will bring to your next relationship, if you are willing to do the work. I encourage you to do the work.

HOW TO WORK WITH THE SACRAL CHAKRA TO ATTRACT MORE LOVE AND GRACE INTO OUR LIVES

One of the essential truths about the Sacral Chakra is knowing that everything we have and everything we do is enough. Finding the appropriate balance between control and letting go is key for this chakra to function well.

When we experience difficult and painful experiences, our bodies get depleted of vital energy, and our reserves run low. If this chakra is not revitalized, it will start to drain the other chakras in order to fill itself. The risk is that the entire energy source of the body can be depleted if we do not nurture and take care of ourselves. That is why moving on from an unfulfilling and unhealthy relationship is essential for your well-being. It is essential to know that you are enough. When we know we are enough, we make better decisions for our overall well-being.

Our relationship to our health and emotional well-being is a reflection of how we honor and take care of ourselves. We need to learn to give our bodies what they need to thrive, such as healthy food, exercise, rest, work, and fun. When we honestly believe we deserve good things, we treat ourselves well. This is an ideal time to give ourselves permission to have the things we need in order to thrive. The more you thrive, the more others around you will thrive.

MY STORY

I find peace in knowing that we both played a part in our marriage and in the dissolution of our marriage; I find comfort in knowing we both did the best we could. The reality is that no sane person makes a commitment to marriage with the intention of sabotaging it and bringing it to a painful closure. After much quietness and reflection, I can clearly see my part in the relationship. The interesting thing is that I thought that by compromising what I needed, giving more and more, and letting disappointments go, I was going to obtain the love and connection my heart was longing for.

The reality is that, by *not* honoring myself and my needs, I ultimately played a role in ending our relationship.

Some of my friends who are ten or twenty years older and obviously blessed with life experience would often say to me, "You do way too much; you're going to burn out." I remember thinking, *They don't know me. I have a ton of energy, and I will be fine.* What I did not realize until now is that they were referring not only to my physical self but also to my emotional and mental self. In the end, I did burn out, and, once I had, there was no turning back for me.

The one thing I do admire about myself is that I do not spend time or energy on blame and making myself right and my partner wrong. I also felt this when my parents passed away while I was fairly young. I never blamed them for anything but rather honored the fact they both did the best that they could. It is a much more peaceful and calm process if you can transition without placing blame. Rather, put your energy into understanding what you can control—and that is *your part* in the relationship.

Do not spend time looking back, because you are not going in that direction. Keep looking forward and being fully present—that is where the beauty of your next chapter will be written.

Positive Affirmations

for the Sacral Chakra

I am grateful for being me.

I am enough just the way I am.

I deserve to be healthy, happy, and in love.

I heal myself when I rest, relax, and honor myself.

Healing happens naturally and effortlessly when I take care of myself.

I love who I am, and I trust that I am exactly where I need to be.

I hold the power to my future by being present and fully engaged in the moment.

STEP 7

FALL IN LOVE WITH THE NEW LIFE THAT AWAITS YOU

Muladhara ✳ Root Chakra

LOCATION: *Tailbone*

STONE: *Red Jasper*

COLOR: *Red*

OIL: *Red Amber*

SOUND: *LAM*

THEME: *Balance*

HEALING PROPERTY:
Grounding, Nourishment

GIFT: *Being Present*

LIFE ISSUE: *Worry*

ARCHETYPE: *Mother Earth*

W*hen you think about the Root Chakra,* envision the roots of a tree. The Root Chakra is the foundation of your entire chakra system and the key to feeling rooted and balanced. It is believed to help you feel grounded to the earth and to feel at home, present, and sturdy. Just like a tree, your Root Chakra supports all your other chakras.

We all experience times in our lives when we feel challenged. Many of us have not been taught how to be resourceful and what tools to use in order to navigate through the changes in our lives. Developing the resources comes from learning how to overcome changes and transitions in our lives. After we experience a huge change, such as divorce, our roots can become compromised, and we struggle to maintain inner and outer balance. Finding a consistent and positive connection to our new reality can help us navigate through our change. Staying present and open to all new possibilities will give you hope for your future.

Focusing your energy on the Root Chakra helps you to experience stillness and peace. It can bring you health, prosperity, and a sense of grounding. What happens when you do not feel rooted? You feel the roots pulling up and a sense of imbalance because you are not grounded—a sense that you could come undone at any time. Loving and taking care of yourself is how you become grounded in your roots. Taking the time to listen to yourself and trusting what you need—and paying attention to what nourishes you—is what keeps you grounded.

Ask yourself "Who am I now?" This is not an ending but a whole new beginning for you. You do not need to let it just "unfold." You can mindfully decide what new path you want for yourself. Your life has now changed, and it is important for you to define where you fit in. You have a wonderful opportunity to connect with the new *you* and build a new life. The experience you have gone through will bring a new *you* to your future. This new *you* has had challenges that will alter how life and future experiences will be viewed. This new, beautiful *you* will come with some new strengths and new vulnerability. Let the new *you* shine—it is through your challenges and setbacks that you truly connect with your authentic self.

Life is a series of natural and spontaneous changes.
Don't resist them. That will only create sorrow.
Let reality be reality; let things flow naturally
forward in whatever way they like.
—Lao Tzu

The key is to become aware of what is important to you *now* and set your intentions on your new goals. Be willing to set the intention but not to be tied to the outcome. Leave room for life to flow effortlessly and spontaneously. Things will unfold, as they should, all in the right time. Allow it to be.

The second powerful question to ask yourself is "What is it that I want with my new life?" This is an ideal time to rewrite your story and recreate the direction you are taking with your life. Meet yourself where you are. Do not try to force the answers. You may not have any answers to the questions for a while. Practice acceptance, and sit with that. Do not judge—just let it be. The only thing that I ask is that you continue to ask yourself these questions on a daily basis. When the time is right and self knows the answers, you will begin to receive them. Honor the process, and let it flow naturally.

Use this new beginning as an opportunity to handle your ex in a new way also. As I am sure you have heard, one definition of insanity is doing things the same way over and over again expecting a new result. Try to handle your ex a little differently, perhaps with a bit more compassion and understanding. If they repeat the behaviors that drove you crazy, do not get upset, aggravated, or angry. Learn to rise above it, and thank the universe for sending you reminders of why you are no longer engaged in a marital relationship with this person. Honor and thank yourself for being strong enough to move on. Remind yourself that this person is doing the best they can.

How can the two of you communicate consciously moving forward? When communicating with your ex and your children, use the following questions to create a new paradigm as you navigate through disagreements with more love and grace.

What are you observing/perceiving?

What are you feeling?

What do you need?

How can I help you?

Do what comes easy. If you are doing something out of obligation, do not do it. Honor yourself and what you need. Only frustration and resentment will arise when you betray what you need.

HOW DO YOU USE THE ROOT CHAKRA TO GET GROUNDED IN YOUR NEW LIFE?

A healthy Root Chakra is strong yet flexible. It is able to adjust to life changes while maintaining a sense of being grounded. Imagine digging up a tree and moving it to a different location. The tree would have to learn to adjust to a new climate, different soil, and new sun exposure in order to survive and thrive. The same goes for you, as your life has been uprooted with your divorce. In order to adjust well to your new life, it will be important to mindfully get grounded in your new reality. It will be important to honor your past, to forgive, to nurture yourself, and to keep your focus on rebuilding and getting grounded in your new reality. This will come by honoring who you are, what you have experienced, and connecting with what you want to create for your new future.

During times of transition, you will need your quiet time as well as your tribe to survive. Your tribe will help you stabilize your Root Chakra during times of change. Since we will be in a new situation, our Root Chakra can become dislocated, and we may initially struggle to maintain inner and outer steadiness. Finding a consistent and steady connection with what is real and true can help us endure and thrive during our transition.

How people treat you is their karma.
How you react is yours.
—WAYNE DYER

It is important to come to terms with the fact that your past has no hold over you. You have the power to make your own interpretations of the situations that have occurred in your life. You have the power to grow and thrive as a result of the lessons you have learned. This new life you are about to embark on will be open to limitless possibilities. In order to successfully launch yourself forward, learn to feed, nourish, and provide for your needs. Start on the path of loving and taking good care of yourself. Learn to listen to, honor, and trust your soul. Pay attention to what fulfills you and makes you feel good. Fill your new life with people and things that nourish you and keep you grounded.

MY STORY

This is a journey, and I have learned many lessons from it. The richness that I have learned from my experience is that I need to honor my heart and soul in order to lead my most authentic life. My instincts and intuition are quite good. I need to learn to trust and honor them. Although my vision has always been a "happily ever after," I have not lost that vision or dream; I just need to create it within a new realm of possibility. I can still have it—it may just look different from what I had originally envisioned.

While divorce and separating my family were not something I had ever envisioned for my life, a lot of growth and richness have come from unwinding my marriage. Most importantly, I listened to my voice, and I honored and took care of myself. It was a huge leap to take, but I had the courage to take it. Through it, the richness that came out for me has been clarity of vision, stronger connection to self, owning my truth, surrendering, intuition, authenticity, peace, facing fears, humbleness, kindness, empathy, and—most of all—a strong sense of hope. I have hope for a loving and graceful transition out of my marriage and hope for a new beginning that honors what I need and want for myself and for my children.

I wish you light, hope and peace as you embark on your journey. May you do so with love and grace.

POSITIVE AFFIRMATIONS

for the Root Chakra

I am exactly where I need to be.

I am grateful for the experiences in my life.

I am grounded and have a strong foundation.

I know that I am truly good.

My roots support me through both good and challenging times.

*I am grateful for the challenges that have taught me
who I truly am.*

When you arrive at your Step 7, allow yourself to...
Reignite~Reinvigorate~Restore~Reinvent~Recharge,
and Reclaim your new life.

I am rooted, and I flow . . .

ABOUT THE AUTHOR

Sylvia Guinan has mastered the ability to find hope and positivity in the most challenging situations. For more than ten years, Sylvia has used her gifts to support people through difficult relationship transitions by helping them to shift from the fear of a failed marriage to a new vision of their life with an empowered beginning.

Her unique experience navigating two divorces in her own life has given Sylvia the tools and skills needed to provide a healing space where couples can unwind their relationship from a loving perspective and create a new story with clarity and authenticity.

As a mother of three, Sylvia's passion is to guide families to be their best selves as they navigate divorce within their own family—from a place of true love and grace.

Additional books by Flower of Life Press

The New Feminine Evolutionary: Embody Presence—Become the Change

Pioneering the Path to Prosperity: Discover the Power of True Wealth and Abundance

Sacred Body Wisdom: Igniting the Flame of Our Divine Humanity

Set Sail: Shine Your Radiance, Activate Your Ascension, Ignite Your Income, Live Your Legacy

Practice: Wisdom from the Downward Dog

Sisterhood of the Mindful Goddess: How to Remove Obstacles, Activate Your Gifts, and Become Your Own Superhero

Path of the Priestess: Discover Your Divine Purpose

Sacred Call of the Ancient Priestess: Birthing a New Feminine Archetype

Rise Above: Free Your Mind One Brushstroke at a Time

Menopause Mavens: Master the Mystery of Menopause

The Power of Essential Oils: Create Positive Transformation in Your Well-Being, Business, and Life

Self-Made Wellionaire: Get Off Your Ass(et), Reclaim Your Health, and Feel Like a Million Bucks

Emerge: 7 Steps to Transformation (No matter what life throws at you!)

Oms From the Mat: Breathe, Move, and Awaken to the Power of Yoga

Oms From the Heart: Open Your Heart to the Power of Yoga

The Four Tenets of Love: Open, Activate, and Inspire Your Life's Path

The Fire-Driven Life: Ignite the Fire of Self-Worth, Health, and Happiness with a Plant-Based Diet

Becoming Enough: A Heroine's Journey to the Already Perfect Self

The Caregiving Journey: Information. Guidance. Inspiration.

Plant-based Vegan & Gluten-free Cooking with Essential Oils

www.floweroflifepress.com

Made in the USA
Middletown, DE
31 July 2020